The Star-Spangled Banner

Written by Douglas M. Rife

Illustrated by Bron Smith

Teaching & Learning Company

1204 Buchanan St., P.O. Box 10
Carthage, IL 62321-0010

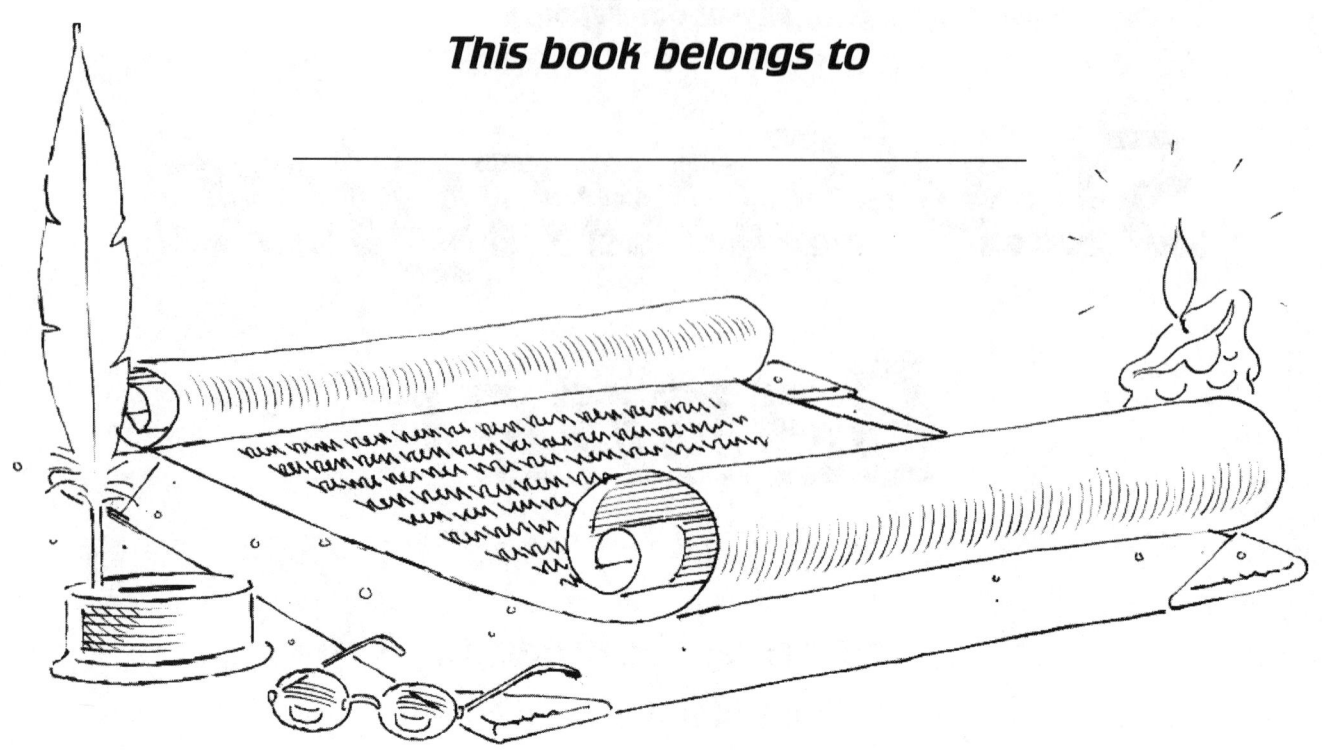

This book belongs to

_____

Cover photo credit to the Smithsonian Institute
National Museum of American History

Copyright © 1998, Teaching & Learning Company

ISBN No. 1-57310-130-3

Printing No. 09876

Teaching & Learning Company
1204 Buchanan St., P.O. Box 10
Carthage, IL 62321-0010

Table of Contents

Objectives. 5

The Colonies   Handout 1 6

Colonial Flags   Handout 2 7

A Brief History of the Flag of the United States   Handout 3 8

State Flags   Handout 4. 9

Flag Test   Handout 5. 10

Receipt for The Star-Spangled Banner   Handout 6 11

Mary Pickersgill, Seamstress of a National Symbol   Handout 7   12

Flag Quiz   Handout 8 13

Flag Word Search   Handout 9 14

The Battle of Baltimore Map   Handout 10. 15

Fort McHenry   Handout 11 16

The Battle of Baltimore   Handout 12. 17

The Battle of Baltimore Map Test   Handout 13 18

By the Dawn's Early Light the Night of
    September 13   Handout 14. 19

Key Questions   Handout 15 20

Francis Scott Key's "The Defense of Fort McHenry"/
    "The Star-Spangled Banner"   Handout 16 21

"The Defense of Fort McHenry"/
    "The Star-Spangled Banner"   Handout 17 22

From Poem to National Song   Handout 18 23

Poem Questions   Handout 19. 25

Blessed Be the Sacred Land   Handout 20 26

Blessed Be the Sacred Land Review   Handout 21 27

God Defend New Zealand   Handout 22. 28

God Defend New Zealand Review   Handout 23 29

The Star-Spangled Banner Today   Handout 24. 30

Bibliography 31

Answer Key 32

Dear Teacher or Parent,

Most people struggle to sing the national anthem. While the grand tune is stirring, it is nonetheless difficult to sing and the words hard to remember. Few realize that the tune is actually an old English drinking song, familiar to most nineteenth-century Americans. The tune has been criticized as a "degenerate barroom tune, a drinking song unworthy of our country's high ideals and standards of patriotism." True or not, the song was an instant hit with Americans. It stirred deep feelings of nationalism in Americans at the end of the War of 1812, considered by many, as America's second war of independence with England.

"The Star-Spangled Banner," however, is not only our national anthem, but also a flag four-stories in length. The history of the two, the flag and the anthem, is inextricably intertwined. That flag, now on display in the Smithsonian Institution in Washington, D.C., flew over Fort McHenry, Baltimore, Maryland, during a 24-hour British siege on a September night during the War of 1812. The next morning, through the fog and the smoke and the mist, it was clear that the flag was still flying over the fort. That was the sign that the British had failed with their ground attack and naval bombardment of Fort McHenry, even though over 1500 shells had been lobbed at the fort. Francis Scott Key, who had to nervously wait on a ship in the harbor during the bombardment, watched all night to see if the flag at the fort was still there. He was so moved at the sight of the flag the next morning, that he was inspired to write the poem, "The Defense of Fort McHenry," that is now our national anthem.

Our young burgeoning nation was a collection of states, fractious at times, with regional interests vying for supremacy. The War of 1812 ended in a draw with the most decisive American victory actually happening after the war had officially ended. Many historians believe Key's poem helped Americans first recognize their national identity.

Today both the poem and the flag are symbols of national pride. By studying the national anthem and the flag that inspired it, students will gain an insight to why the poem became the national song. They will also gain an understanding to what symbols mean in a modern society. The activities in this unit have two parts—narrative and review. Students first read the narratives and then review the material through a variety of activities, including crossword puzzles, mapping activities and questions and answers that test for comprehension and understanding. The activities are designed to work together as one unit but may also be used alone.

Through these narratives and activities, students will learn about the history of flags in America, the history of the flag, "The Star-Spangled Banner," the battle for Fort McHenry and the history of the poem "The Defense of Fort McHenry" which became our national song. Students will also compare our national song to Pakistan's and New Zealand's. Students will soon understand that flags have history sewn right into them!

Sincerely,

Douglas

Douglas M. Rife

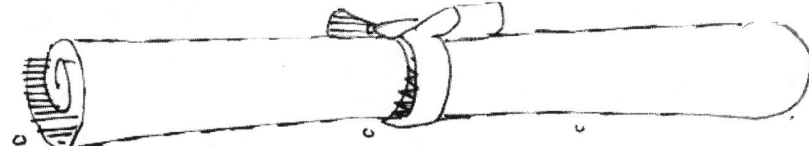

Objectives

After completing the following activities	the students should be able to ...
The Colonies **Colonial Flags** **A Brief History of the Flag of the United States** **State Flags** **Flag Test**	1. explain the history of the United States flag 2. understand the symbolism of the flag as a national symbol
Receipt for the Star-Spangled Banner **Mary Pickersgill, Seamstress of a National Symbol** **Flag Quiz** **Flag Crossword**	1. understand the history of the flag and the Star-Spangled Banner 2. answer questions using a primary source document 3. sequence the events of September 13 and 14
The Battle of Baltimore Map **Fort McHenry** **The Battle of Baltimore** **The Battle of Baltimore Map Test** **By the Dawn's Early Light . . .** **Key Questions**	1. explain the details of the Battle of Baltimore 2. map the events 3. sequence the events of September 13 and 14
Francis Scott Key's "The Star-Spangled Banner" **The Star-Spangled Banner** **From Poem to National Song** **Poem Questions** **Blessed Be the Sacred Land Review** **God Defend New Zealand Review** **The Star-Spangled Banner Today**	1. repeat the words of the national anthem 2. synthesize the history of the national anthem 3. compare and contrast the U.S. national anthem and the Pakistani national anthem 4. compare and contrast the U.S. national anthem and the New Zealand national anthem

The Colonies

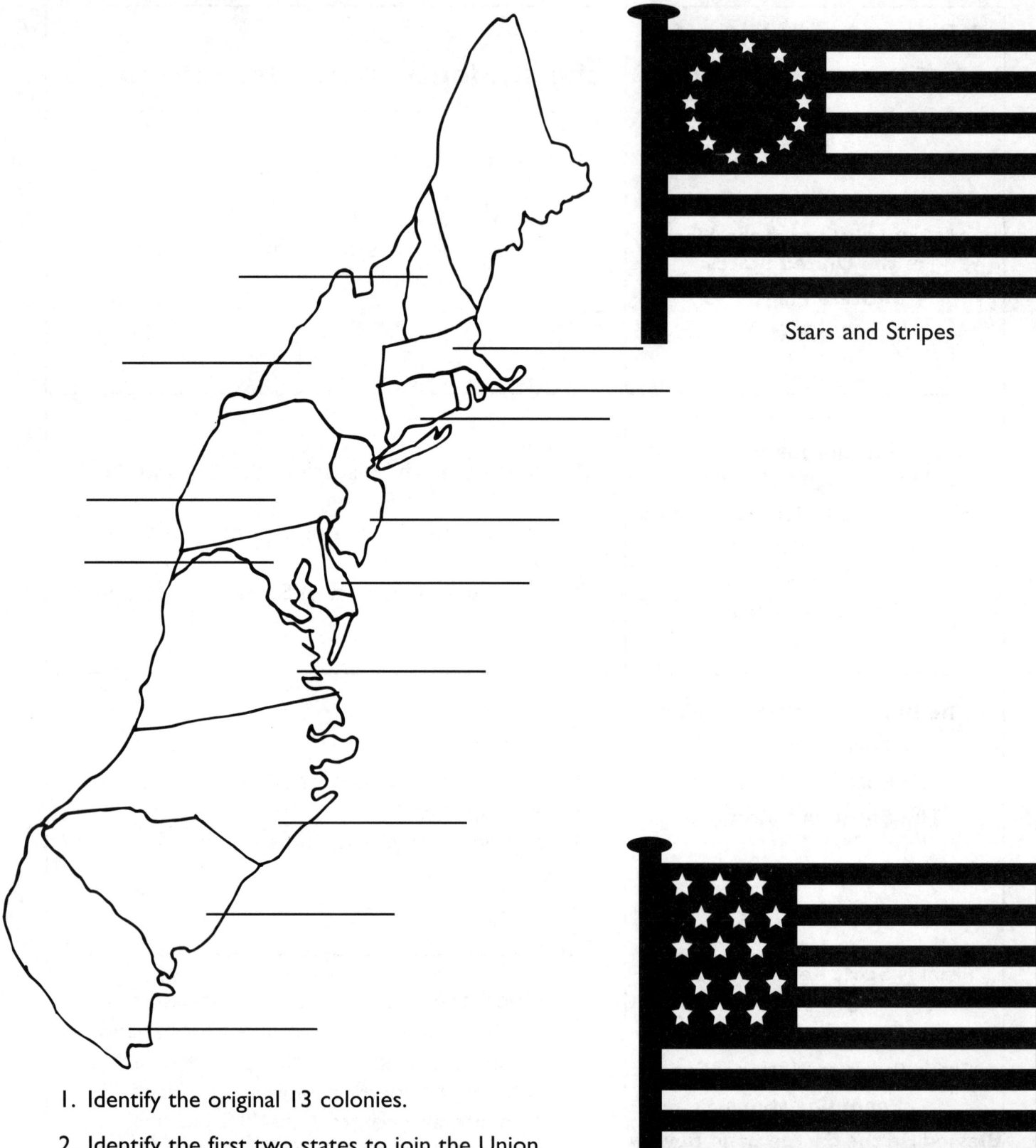

Stars and Stripes

Star-Spangled Banner

1. Identify the original 13 colonies.

2. Identify the first two states to join the Union.

3. Research those two states and write the admission dates next to the state name.

Colonial Flags

Length

Top (head)

Canton

Width

Fly

Hoist

Bottom (foot)

Taunton Flag

The Taunton flag first flew in Taunton, Massachusetts, in 1774. The Union Jack with the words *Liberty and Union* were sewn into the scarlet field.

William Moultrie Flag

This flag of blue, designed by William Moultrie, with the white crescent in the canton, and white type *Liberty*, spoke simply to the message of the revolution. This flag was flown over Fort Sullivan during the British attack on June 28, 1776.

Gadsden Flag

This was a bright yellow banner with a coiled rattlesnake in the field with the words *DON'T TREAD ON ME* emblazoned across the bottom. The rattlesnake, a symbol on several revolutionary flags, represented the colonial readiness to strike against the British.

Bunker Hill Flag

This flag displayed St. George's red cross in the canton with a pine tree in the first quarter of the cross. The pine tree, also minted on all Massachusetts' coinage, symbolized the tree under which the famous Sons of Liberty met.

Taunton Flag, 1774

William Moultrie Flag, 1776

Gadsden Flag, 1776

Bunker Hill Flag, 1775

A Brief History of the Flag of the United States

Union Jack, 1606

Grand Union Flag

Stars and Stripes

Star-Spangled Banner

No other symbol of the United States is as revered as the United States' flag and few are as old. Like many of our institutions, the founders of our country borrowed from England to build the foundations of the new government—that was true of the flag as well.

Union Jack

The United States began as a colony of Great Britain. Great Britain had a great influence on our history including our flag and its history. The British Union Jack is a mix of two flags—the flag of Scotland (St. Andrew's Cross) and the flag of England (St. George's Cross). In 1606, when England and Scotland became one nation, King James I merged the two to form one flag.

Grand Union Flag

The first flag of the United States, sometimes called the Cambridge Flag, combines the Union Jack of Great Britain with the stripes. The Union Jack in the canton of the flag reminds us of the influence of Great Britain in our heritage. The stripes represent the 13 colonies. Washington raised this flag in January of 1776 at Cambridge, Massachusetts.

Stars and Stripes

On June 14, 1777, the Continental Congress passed a resolution declaring "that the flag of the thirteen United States be thirteen stripes alternating red and white; that the union be thirteen stars, white in a blue field, representing a new constellation." The stars in the field represent only one arrangement that was popular during the revolution.

Star-Spangled Banner

Vermont and Kentucky were the first two states added to the Union after the original 13, When they were admitted not only were two stars added to the flag, but also two stripes. This was the flag of the United States from 1795 until 1818. In April 1818, Congress passed a law returning to the tradition of the United States flag with 13 stripes. Congress realized that adding a stripe with each additional state would soon make the flag an unusual shape. So, Congress provided for a new star to be added for each new state admitted to the Union.

State Flags

Maryland State Flag

Maryland State Flag (adopted March 9, 1904)

One of the earliest uses of flags was as a mark of heraldry. The Maryland state flag has the distinction of displaying the arms of the Baltimore families, founding families of the state. The first and fourth quarters of black and yellow diamonds represent the Calvert family; the second and third, red and white crosses, represent the Crossland family.

Texas State Flag

Texas State Flag (adopted January 25, 1839)

The first flag of Texas was a blue field with one five-point white star with the word *TEXAS* spelled out, a letter at each star point. In 1836, the lone star was centered on a blue vertical field with two horizontal stripes, one red, one white. The red represents courage and the blood shed for Texas; white represents purity; and blue symbolizes loyalty, justice and truth.

Hawaii State Flag

Hawaii State Flag (adopted May 20, 1845)

The Union Jack in the canton of the Hawaiian flag dates back to King Kamehameha I. Hawaii was a British protectorate in 1794. Eight red, white and blue alternating stripes represent the eight islands of Hawaii, Maui, Oahu, Kauai, Molokai, Lanai, Niihau and Kahoolawe. The blue represents loyalty, truth and justice; red represents courage; and white signifies purity.

Iowa State Flag

Iowa State Flag (adopted March 29, 1921)

The flag is divided into three vertical panels of blue, white and red, just as the French tricolor, reminding Iowans that the state, as part of the Louisiana Territory, once belonged to France. On the white panel in the center, an eagle holds a banner that reads "Our Liberty We Prize, and Our Rights We Will Maintain." The red represents courage; white symbolizes purity; and blue represents loyalty, justice and truth.

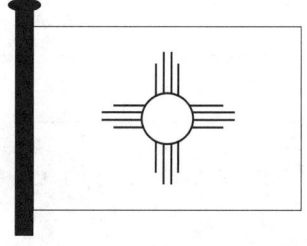

New Mexico State Flag

New Mexico State Flag (adopted March 19, 1925)

The gold color of the field and the red of the design represent the colors of Queen Isabella of Castille, representing Spanish rule. The Zia Pueblo symbol, in the center of the flag, represents the sun, the one source of power.

Name _____

Flag Test
Flag Match
Match the letter of the flag to the picture.

a. Gadsden Flag
b. Grand Union Flag
c. Hawaii State Flag
d. Star-Spangled Banner
e. New Mexico State Flag
f. Bunker Hill Flag

1. _____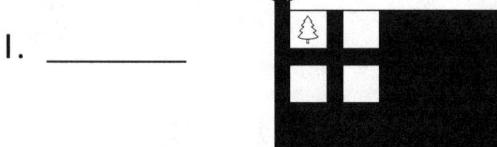

2. _____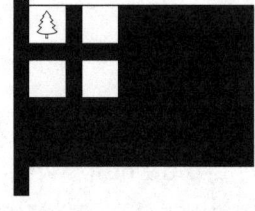

3. _____

4. _____

5. _____

6. _____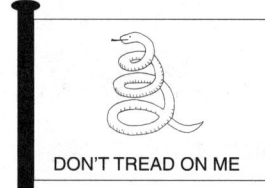

DON'T TREAD ON ME

Flag Questions
Look at the flags above and answer the following questions:

1. What does the rattlesnake represent? _____

_____

2. Which state flag indicates, through its symbolism, that the state was once ruled by France?

_____

3. In what two ways is the Star-Spangled Banner different than the U.S. flag of today? _____

_____

4. What does the pine tree represent? _____

_____

5. Explain what the circle with the four sets of lines represents? What is the origin of this

symbol? _____

_____

Receipt for The Star-Spangled Banner

Reproduced by permission of The Star-Spangled Banner Flag House and Museum, Baltimore, Maryland.

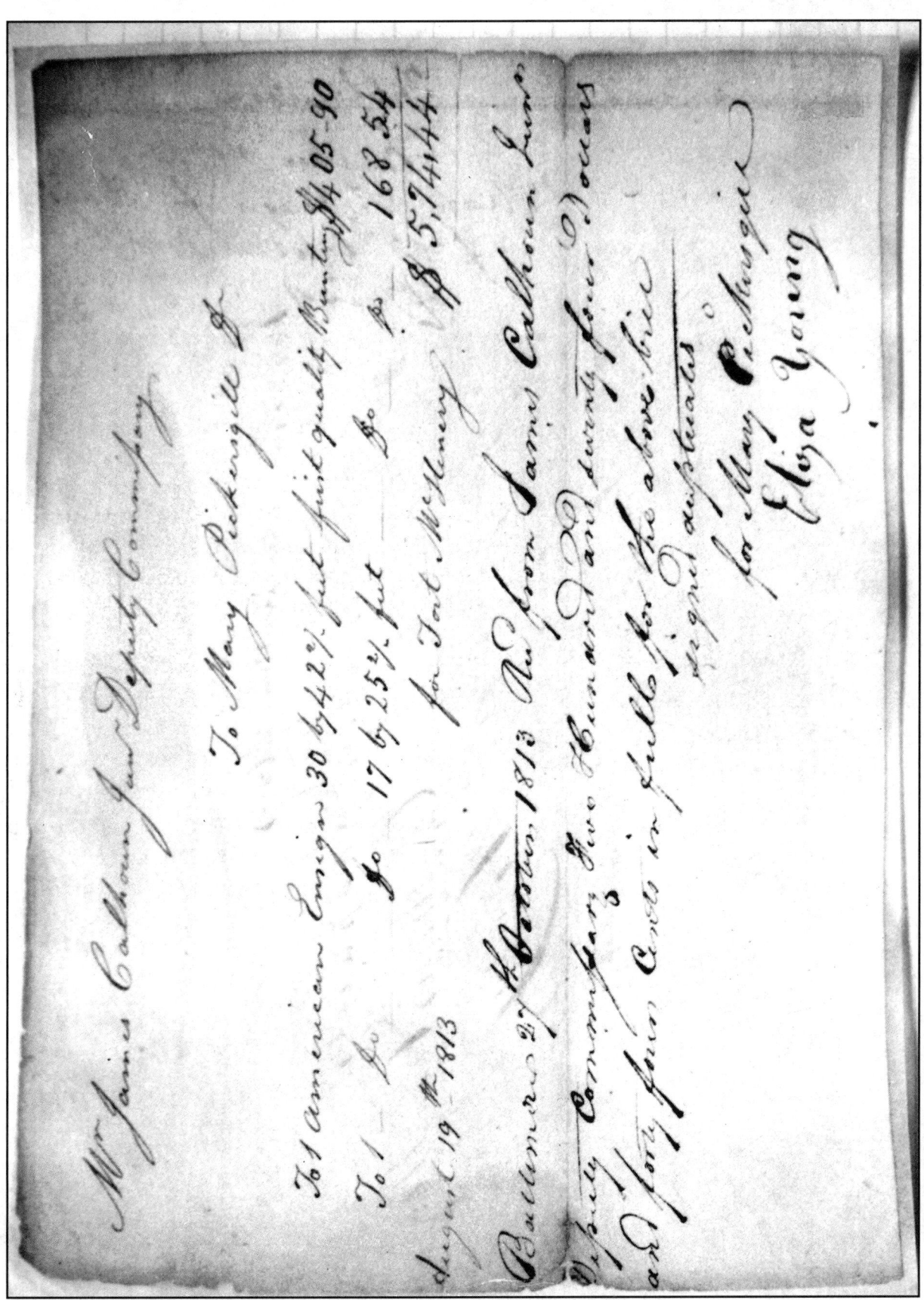

Mary Pickersgill, Seamstress of a National Symbol

Reproduced by permission from The Star-Spangled Banner Flag House and Museum, Baltimore, Maryland.

The History of the Star-Spangled Banner

The commanders of Fort McHenry knew almost certainly that the British fleet would make their way down the Chesapeake Bay to attack the city of Baltimore. The city was defended by Fort McHenry, which lay at the mouth of the Northwest Branch, the channel leading to Baltimore.

Knowing that a battle would ensue at Fort McHenry for the defense of Baltimore, the commanders decided to have a large flag sewn for the Fort. Major George Armistead's boast was that he wanted the flag to be big enough "that the British will have no difficulty in seeing it from a distance."

In August of 1813, Mary Pickersgill was contracted to sew "1 American Ensign 30 by 42 feet first quality Bunting $405.90." This was to be the largest American flag flown in the country up to that point—over four stories in length.

Mary and her 12-year-old daughter, Caroline, sewed the flag on the floor of a Baltimore brewery during July and August of 1813.

Name _____

Flag Quiz

Read the receipt and answer the following questions:

1. To whom is the receipt made out? _____

2. What is an "American Ensign"? _____

3. How many flags did this receipt purchase? _____

4. How much was paid for each flag? _____

5. What sizes were the flags? _____

6. For whom were the flags sewn? _____

7. What was the total amount paid to the seamstress? _____

Beyond the Receipt

1. Legend tells us that Betsy Ross sewed the Stars and Stripes Flag of 1777. Research to find out what primary source documents exist to support that claim.

2. Compare the claim that Betsy Ross sewed the Stars and Stripes Flag of 1777 to the claim that Mary Pickersgill sewed the Star-Spangled Banner.

Handout 8

Name _____

Flag Word Search

Find the words in the word bank hidden in the puzzle. Look up, down, diagonally and backwards.

```
T  H  E  K  O  S  T  L  L  I  G  S  R  E  K  C  I  P  Y  R  A  M
A  H  I  G  B  M  K  J  M  E  E  J  O  Y  Y  A  N  N  R  I  E  D
N  A  E  B  R  S  E  M  A  J  E  E  E  E  J  R  O  H  J  A  R  B
O  N  G  S  I  E  M  T  Q  U  A  K  K  S  U  O  A  V  I  B  U  R
I  E  N  C  T  L  C  D  V  O  T  T  A  E  D  L  S  I  E  L  J  M
N  D  W  A  I  A  V  E  E  T  T  S  T  P  Y  I  E  A  P  Q  N  C
U  H  O  P  E  O  R  N  O  O  H  U  H  T  A  N  N  I  P  A  F  A
D  T  K  E  L  L  Y  S  C  A  R  T  Y  E  U  E  C  H  O  O  R  D
N  J  E  I  T  S  R  S  P  N  S  G  E  M  S  U  A  N  R  D  O  M
A  E  W  S  O  I  S  K  I  A  H  L  V  B  O  W  S  T  Q  O  N  I
R  K  I  G  L  I  E  O  L  H  N  L  U  E  N  I  M  A  P  U  T  R
G  R  A  M  C  O  G  G  Y  A  R  G  I  R  O  C  U  T  X  G  K  A
N  X  A  N  N  N  R  L  O  C  M  A  L  A  H  O  B  E  I  L  C  L
Z  D  A  J  I  G  E  N  O  T  S  L  R  E  U  Y  U  R  M  A  A  C
F  R  Z  H  S  I  T  I  R  B  A  F  N  I  D  G  E  E  O  S  J  O
F  C  K  S  I  M  L  T  E  O  W  R  I  B  X  B  J  S  N  R  N  C
K  X  B  H  L  O  S  P  T  A  Y  N  O  S  I  D  A  M  U  H  O  H
E  I  W  A  R  M  O  N  R  O  E  F  E  R  N  X  I  N  T  O  I  R
L  O  C  H  N  I  J  B  Q  D  S  X  R  L  F  A  B  A  N  N  A  N
A  L  E  P  U  T  S  M  R  U  Y  O  I  N  W  M  E  E  S  E  U  N
Z  A  T  H  E  B  A  T  T  L  E  O  F  B  A  L  T  I  M  O  R  E
```

Word Bank

Admiral Cochrane	Grand Union
The Battle of Baltimore	James
British	Madison
Caroline	Mary Pickersgill
Dr. Beanes	Monroe
flag	September
Fort McHenry	The Star-Spangled Banner
Francis Scott Key	Union Jack

14   *Handout 9*   TLC10130 Copyright © Teaching & Learning Company, Carthage, IL 62321-0010

The Battle of Baltimore Map

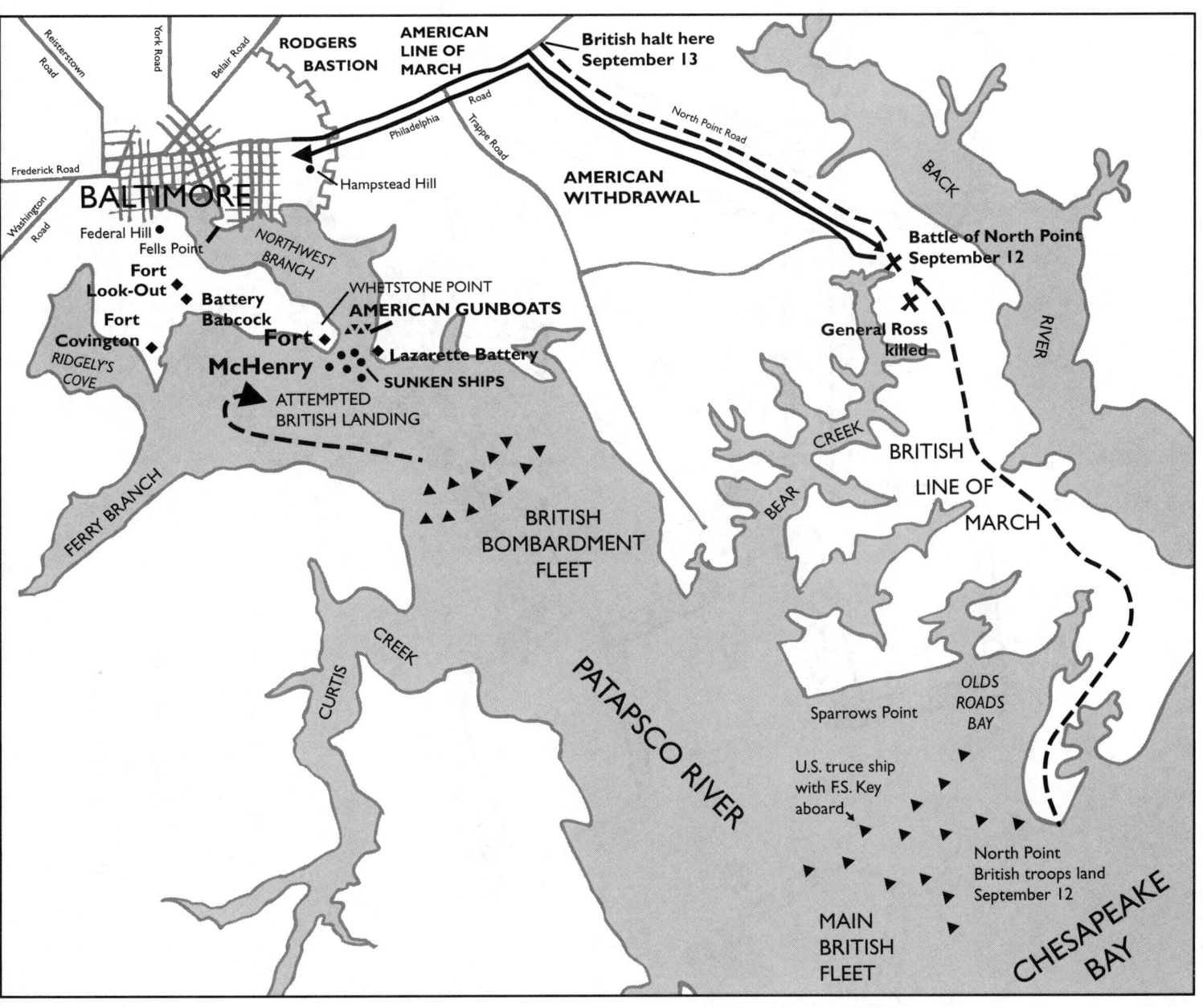

Reisterstown Road

York Road

Belair Road

RODGERS BASTION

AMERICAN LINE OF MARCH

British halt here September 13

Philadelphia Road

Trappe Road

North Point Road

AMERICAN WITHDRAWAL

BACK

Frederick Road

Washington Road

BALTIMORE

Hampstead Hill

Federal Hill

Fells Point

NORTHWEST BRANCH

Fort Look-Out

Battery Babcock

WHETSTONE POINT

AMERICAN GUNBOATS

Battle of North Point September 12

Fort Covington

RIDGELY'S COVE

Fort McHenry

Lazarette Battery

SUNKEN SHIPS

General Ross killed

RIVER

ATTEMPTED BRITISH LANDING

BRITISH LINE OF MARCH

FERRY BRANCH

CREEK

BEAR

BRITISH BOMBARDMENT FLEET

CURTIS CREEK

PATAPSCO RIVER

OLDS ROADS BAY

Sparrows Point

U.S. truce ship with F.S. Key aboard

North Point British troops land September 12

MAIN BRITISH FLEET

CHESAPEAKE BAY

—————— American troop movements

- - - - - - British troop movements

Fort McHenry

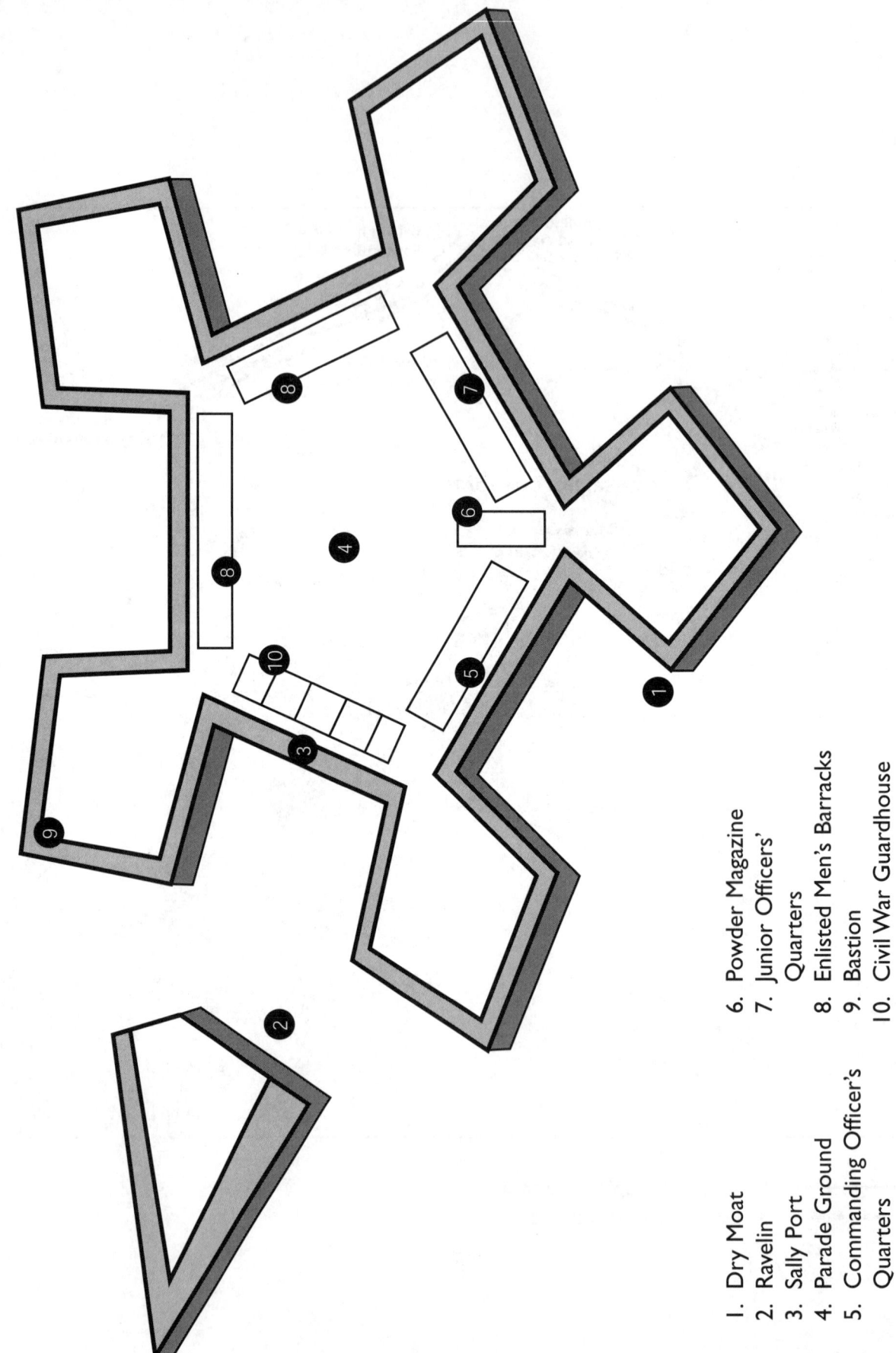

1. Dry Moat
2. Ravelin
3. Sally Port
4. Parade Ground
5. Commanding Officer's Quarters
6. Powder Magazine
7. Junior Officers' Quarters
8. Enlisted Men's Barracks
9. Bastion
10. Civil War Guardhouse

The Battle of Baltimore

The battle for the harbor, Fort McHenry and the city of Baltimore had been anticipated. The summer of 1814 had been a bad one for American forces during the War of 1812. In April of 1814, the British defeated Napoleon and began to concentrate on fighting the Americans, which up to that time had been little more than bothersome. By the middle of August, a British expeditionary force had landed in Maryland. They had marched on Washington, D.C., and set fire to it. President Madison's wife, Dolley, barely made it out of the White House before the British arrived. She managed to cut out the famous Gilbert Stuart painting of George Washington and fled before the British entered a practically deserted city.

British General Robert Ross led the force that torched Washington, D.C. The next target was Baltimore. Unlike Washington, however, Baltimore was prepared. Senator Samuel Smith had organized the military and volunteer forces around the city. Defenses were put up everywhere. Major George Armistead commanded the American forces at the star-shaped Fort McHenry, which lay guarding the channel that was the waterway to Baltimore. American troops sunk ship hulls at the opening to the Northwest Branch River to help blockade the British fleet from entering the city's harbor. American gunboats were anchored behind the ship hulls. The area marshaled over 15,000 men from Maryland, Pennsylvania and Virginia to combat the British. The city and the fort were ready for a fight.

On September 12, part of the British fleet anchored at the mouth of the Patapsco River on the edge of the Chesapeake Bay. The British bombardment fleet moved in closer, so ship artillery could reach Fort McHenry. British General Robert Ross landed his troops on the tip of North Point and vowed to march his army to eat supper that night in either Baltimore or Hell. Ross and his troops began the march, a total of 12 miles, to Baltimore. They had marched nearly halfway to Baltimore, at the head of Bear Creek, when they encountered American forces. The Battle of North Point ensued. A sharpshooter picked off a British officer from his white stallion mortally wounding him, it turned out to be General Ross. The troops continued to advance forward but were stopped where North Point Road intersects with Philadelphia Road.

Admiral Cochrane began bombardment of Fort McHenry at dawn of September 13, which lasted 24 hours. It was estimated that over 1500 shells, some of them weighing as much as 250 pounds, were fired at the fort. The bombardment produced a spectacular light show in the night sky.

Fort McHenry withstood the bombardment and the American troops repelled the British troops on the ground, forcing a British retreat. At 7 a.m. on September 14, the British withdrew. The Star-Spangled Banner was still flying over Fort McHenry.

Name _____

The Battle of Baltimore Map Test

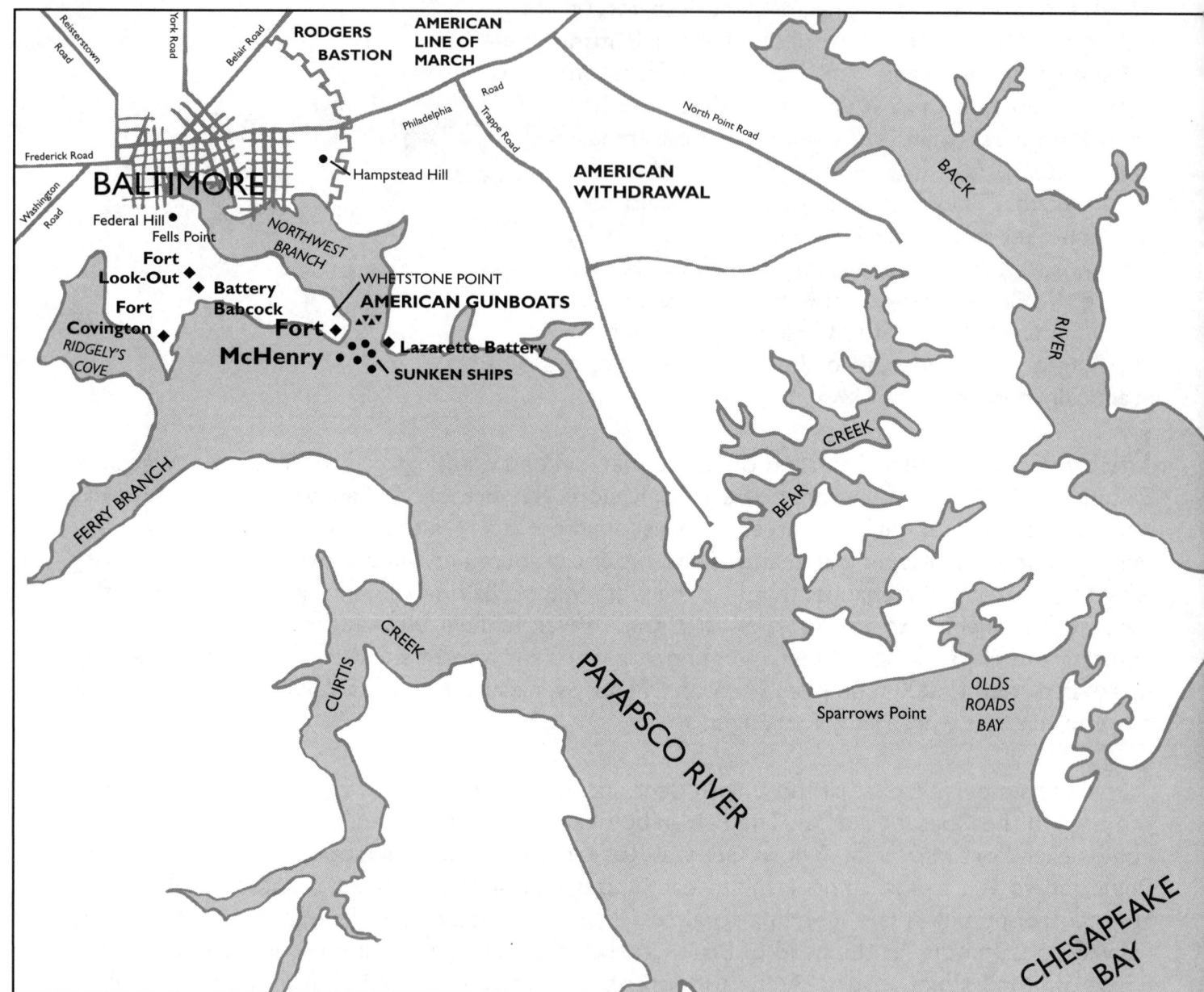

1. Draw a line from where the British land forces landed to where they were halted.
2. Mark on the map with an X where the Battle of North Point took place.
3. Indicate with two Xs where the British land troops were halted.
4. Using three Xs, indicate where the main British fleet lay in the harbor.
5. Using four Xs, indicate where the British bombardment forces were situated.
6. Circle the place where the truce ship was anchored that carried Francis Scott Key.

By the Dawn's Early Light the Night of September 13

Francis Scott Key was born in Frederick County (now Carroll County), Maryland, on August 1, 1779. He graduated from St. Johns College and moved to Georgetown, D.C., in 1802 to practice law. Key wrote poetry in his spare time. In fact, some of his poems were published in 1857. He was a U.S. attorney for the District of Columbia from 1833 to 1841, but will always be remembered for his poem "The Defense of Fort McHenry." And if it had not been for his friend, Dr. William Beanes, Francis Scott Key might never have written the poem.

Throughout the summer of 1814, the British were attacking the American seaports and mainland without impunity. They had rousted the Americans out of their own capitol, Washington, D.C., in August and were moving southward by sea toward Baltimore. The British were so emboldened by their victories that Admiral George Cochrane informed the American Secretary of State, James Monroe, that his navy and land forces had chosen Fort McHenry as their next target for demolition.

As the British troops moved south, a few of the stragglers found themselves in a donnybrook in a Maryland tavern. Dr. Beanes led a local citizen group to jail the offending British soldiers and found himself arrested after being charged with attacking a British soldier with his pistol. After his capture he was taken aboard the *Surprise* which was anchored in the Baltimore Harbor.

Francis Scott Key, after hearing of the debacle, made his way to the fleet to secure Dr. Beanes' release. Key and another friend, John S. Skinner, carried a note with them from President James Madison to secure the good doctor's release. Negotiation went slowly. Admiral Cochrane at first refused Key's pleas for Dr. Beanes' freedom. Key, a young lawyer from Georgetown, argued passionately for leniency, knowing full well that the usual punishment for a crime of this nature, would be hanging. The British were convinced that the doctor had reneged on his promise of neutrality. But Key convinced Cochrane to spare Beanes' life because he had given wounded British soldiers excellent care.

Armed with letters from British soldiers, Key convinced the Admiral to relent. Cochrane, however, was in the final preparations for the bombardment of Fort McHenry. Because Key, Skinner and Beanes had seen the British fleet preparing for the attack, Cochrane did not allow them to return to land. He ordered them back to their ship, the *Minden*, where they were to stay.

The bombardment began the morning of September 13th, and as the poem says, by the dawn's early light (of the next day) Key could still see the flag. Even after the British had lobbed over 1500 shells, some as heavy as 250 pounds, Fort McHenry had not fallen. Key was moved by the moment and began to write his poem, which he finished later that night at the Indian Queen Hotel.

Name _____

Key Questions

Matching

Match the letter to the correct description on the right.

a. Francis Scott Key   _____   1. British commander

b. Dr. William Beanes   _____   2. Arrested by the British

c. Admiral Cochrane   _____   3. Secretary of State

d. James Monroe   _____   4. Authored "The Defense of Fort McHenry"

e. James Madison   _____   5. U.S. President

Key Questions

Read the descriptions, "The Battle of Baltimore" and "By the Dawn's Early Light . . ." and study the drawing of Fort McHenry. Then answer the following questions:

1. Why was Francis Scott Key held during the bombardment of Fort McHenry? _____

   _____

2. Which British General was killed by American sharpshooters the night of September

   12, 1814? _____

3. How many shells were fired upon Fort McHenry? _____

4. Why was Dr. Beanes given leniency by Admiral Cochrane? _____

   _____

5. Who won the Battle of Fort McHenry? _____

   _____

6. What inspired Francis Scott Key? _____

   _____

Francis Scott Key's "The Defense of Fort McHenry"/"The Star-Spangled Banner"

Reproduced by permission of the Maryland Historical Society, Baltimore.

"The Defense of Fort McHenry"/ "The Star-Spangled Banner"

Oh! say, can you see, by the dawn's early light,
What so proudly we hailed at the twilight's last gleaming?
Whose broad stripes and bright stars through the perilous fight,
O'er the ramparts we watched were so gallantly streaming?
And the rockets' red glare, the bombs bursting in air,
Gave proof through the night that our flag was still there.
Oh! say, does that star-spangled banner yet wave
O'er the land of the free and the home of the brave?

On the shore, dimly seen through the mist of the deep,
Where the foe's haughty host in dread silence resposes,
What is that which the breeze, o'er the towering steep,
As it fitfully blows, half conceals, half discloses?
Now it catches the gleam of the morning's first beam,
In full glory reflected, now shines on the stream.
'Tis the star-spangled banner. Oh! long may it wave
O'er the land of the free and the home of the brave!

And where is that band who so vauntingly swore
That the havoc of war and the battle's confusion
A home and a country should leave us no more?
Their blood has washed out their foul footstep's pollution.
No refuge could save the hireling and slave
From the terror of flight or the gloom of the grave,
And the star-spangled banner in triumph doth wave
O'er the land of the free and the home of the brave.

Oh! thus be it ever when freemen shall stand
Between their loved home and the war's desolation,
Blest with vict'ry and peace, may the Heav'n-rescued land
Praise the Pow'r that hath made and preserved us a nation.
Then conquer we must, when our cause it is just,
And this be our motto—"In God is our trust."
And the star-spangled banner in triumph shall wave
O'er the land of the free and the home of the brave.

Handout 17

From Poem to National Song
The History of
"The Star-Spangled Banner"
The National Anthem

Reprinted with permission from the Maryland Historical Society, Baltimore.

After the battle was over, the British fleet pulled up anchor and sailed out of the harbor. The *Minden* and her passengers were then free to sail back to Baltimore.

Key had begun writing "The Defense of Fort McHenry" almost as soon as the smoke cleared away from the flag. Through the mist, fog, smoke and haze, Key saw the enormous flag hanging limply from the fort's flagpole and set his pen to paper. He had the first stanza of the poem written and in his coat pocket before he was back in his hotel room. The next three verses were written quickly.

Later that night, Key showed his brother-in-law, Judge Joseph H. Nicholsen, his poem. Nicholsen took it immediately to the printing office of Benjamin Edes, where a young apprentice named Samuel Sands, set the poem in type.

Judge Nicholsen suggested that the poem could be sung to the tune of "Anacreon in Heaven," a song familiar to Americans at that time. "Anacreon in Heaven" was composed in England in the 1770s and was widely sung in taverns throughout America. It was very likely that Key and Nicholsen were well acquainted with the tune. That very night the handbills with the poem were distributed, it was a success. In fact, as the British fleet sailed out of the harbor, stage actor Ferdinand Durang sang the song to an enthusiastic and cheering crowd in a Baltimore tavern, the night of September 14th.

By September 20th, the *Baltimore Patriot* printed the song in the newspaper. As early as 1815, the poem, "The Defense of Fort McHenry" was known as "The Star-Spangled Banner." The song soon became a favorite. John Philip Sousa pronounced it a great march with great spirit. National anthem contests were held sporadically, first in 1861 as a publicity stunt by none other than P.T. Barnum. No other song garnered stronger support than "The Star-Spangled Banner." By 1889, it had become the unofficial anthem. The navy played it at flag raisings on its ships. As early as 1903, the army had adopted it, as well. President Woodrow Wilson proclaimed it to be the national anthem, and finally on March 3, 1931, after a long campaign by the Veterans of Foreign Wars, the United States Congress proclaimed "The Star-Spangled Banner" as the official national anthem of the United States.

Handout 18

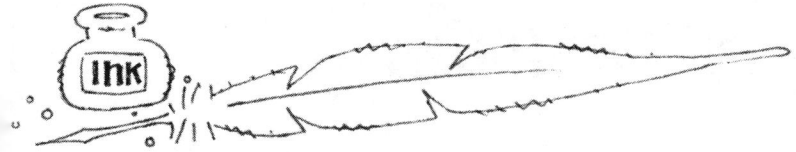

Poem Questions

Read "The Star-Spangled Banner" and the "From Poem to National Song" handouts and answer the following questions:

1. What does the poem say we proudly hailed? _____

_____

2. What are ramparts? _____

3. What was lighting the night sky? _____

_____

4. To which part of the flag does the "star-spangled" refer? _____

_____

5. How many stars were there on the Star-Spangled Banner? _____

_____

6. How does that compare to the flag of today? _____

_____

7. What do the stars on the flag represent? _____

_____

8. How many stripes were there on the Star-Spangled Banner flag of 1812? _____

9. What did the stripes represent? _____

10. Describe how the poem is personal to Francis Scott Key. _____

_____

11. Where does the tune for the song "The Star-Spangled Banner" come from? _____

_____

12. When did "The Star-Spangled Banner" become the official national anthem of the United States? _____

Beyond the Anthem

1. Which song do you think should be the national anthem? Why?

2. Many critics have written their opinions of the national anthem. Write a musical review of "The Star-Spangled Banner."

3. On the back of this sheet, write a poem to replace "The Star-Spangled Banner."

Blessed Be the Sacred Land
The National Anthem of Pakistan
(translation)

Blessed be the **sacred** land
Happy be the **bounteous** realm,
Symbol of high resolve, Land of Pakistan,
Blessed be thou **citadel** of faith.
The Order of this Sacred Land
Is the might of the brotherhood of the people.
May the nation, the country, and the state
Shine in glory everlasting.
Blessed be the goal of our ambition.
This flag of the **Crescent and the Star**
Leads the way to progress and perfection,
Interpreter of our past, glory of our present,
Inspiration of our future,
Symbol of Almighty's protection.

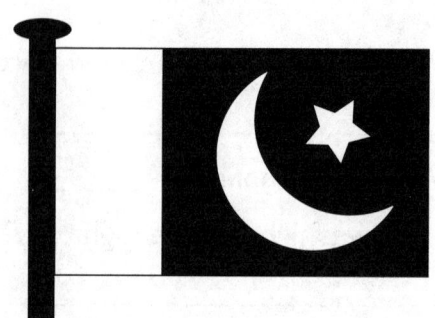

Pakistan Flag (adopted August 14, 1947)

The symbol of Islam, the white crescent and the star, is displayed on a tartan green field that is three-quarters of the flag, representing the Muslim majority of Pakistan. The white vertical panel represents the country's religious minority.

Blessed Be the Sacred Land
The National Anthem of Pakistan Review

Vocabulary

sacred
declared to be holy

bounteous
plentiful, abundant

citadel
a fortress, or stronghold

crescent and the star
a symbol of Islam

Read "The National Anthem of Pakistan" and answer the following questions:

1. Name the five references to religious values in the anthem. _____

   _____

2. How does Pakistan's national anthem commit people to the faith? _____

   _____

3. Read the words to "The Star-Spangled Banner." How does the U.S. national anthem compare to Pakistan's national anthem? How are the two different? _____

   _____

4. How are they the same? _____

   _____

God Defend New Zealand
The National Anthem of New Zealand

1. God of nations at thy feet
   In the bonds of love we meet.
   Hear our voices, we entreat,
   God defend our free land.
   Guard Pacific's triple star
   From the Shafts of strife and war,
   Make her praises heard afar,
   God defend New Zealand.

2. Men of every **creed** and race
   Gather here before thy face,
   Asking thee to bless this place,
   God defend our free land.
   From **dissension**, envy, hate,
   And corruption guard our state,
   Make our country good and great,
   God defend New Zealand.

3. Peace, not war, shall be our boast,
   But should foes **assail** our coast,
   Make us then a mighty host,
   God defend our free land.
   Lord of battles in thy might,
   Put our enemies to flight,
   Let our cause be just and right,
   God defend New Zealand.

4. Let our love of Thee increase,
   May thy blessings never cease,
   Give us plenty, give us peace,
   God defend our free land.
   From dishonour and from shame
   Guard our country's spotless name,
   Crown her with immortal fame,
   God defend New Zealand.

5. May our mountains ever be
   Freedom's **ramparts** on the sea,
   Make us faithful unto thee,
   God defend our free land.
   Guide her in the nation's van,
   Preaching love and true to man,
   Working out thy glorious plan.
   God defend New Zealand.

New Zealand Flag (adopted June 12, 1902)

Representing New Zealand's British heritage, the Union Jack is displayed in the flag's canton. Red stars outlined in white form the constellation, the Southern Cross, in a field of deep blue.

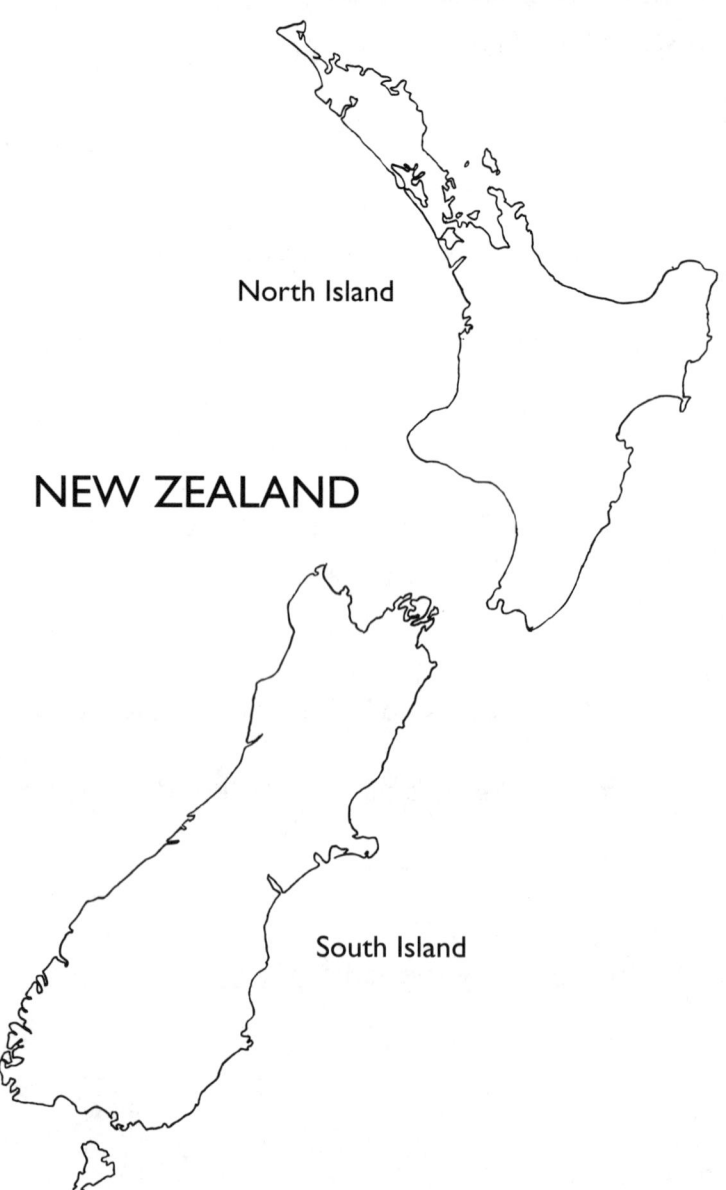

North Island

NEW ZEALAND

South Island

God Defend New Zealand
The National Anthem of New Zealand
Review

Vocabulary

creed
religious beliefs

dissension
discard

assail
to attack

ramparts
a fortification used to protect

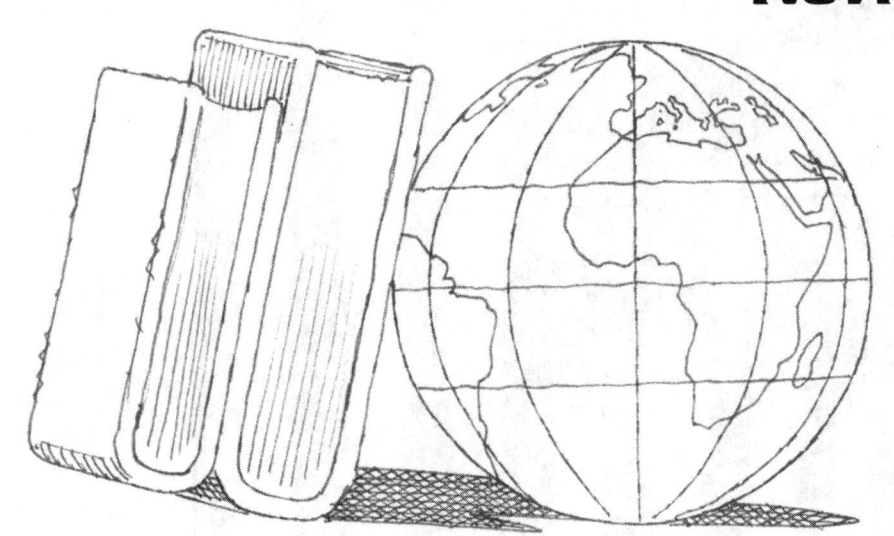

1. What is the refrain? _____

_____

2. How many references are there to God in the song? _____

_____

3. What do you think this means about the country? _____

_____

4. Explain how mountains could be used as ramparts. _____

_____

5. Compare New Zealand's national anthem to Pakistan's. _____

_____

6. How are they alike? _____

_____

7. How are they different? _____

_____

8. How are the two different from the U.S. national anthem? _____

_____

The Star-Spangled Banner Today

The most famous American flag is without question the Star-Spangled Banner. The flag was the inspiration for our national anthem and Americans consider it an icon of freedom. The flag was originally 30 by 42 feet, the largest to fly in the country up to that time.

The Star-Spangled Banner has, though, been reduced in size. Today the flag is now 34 feet in length, instead of the original 42 feet! During the battle, the flag was hit 11 times. After the battle, material from the flag was used to wrap one of the fallen defenders killed during the bombardment of Fort McHenry, Baltimore, Maryland. The flag was also so dear to people that up until the twentieth century, Americans were allowed to clip off pieces of the flag as souvenirs. From 1815 until 1907, eight feet of the length of the flag was snipped.

In 1912, Eben Appleton, Colonel Armistead's grandson, presented the tattered Star-Spangled Banner to the Smithsonian Institution in Washington, D.C. The flag has been slowly deteriorating even further. The cotton and wool fibers have become fragile from continued exposure to ultraviolet lights and pollutants in the air. Like other artifacts that have great historical significance to our country, however, scientists are trying to do everything they can to preserve the Star-Spangled Banner for future generations to see.

The Declaration of Independence and the Constitution, our founding documents, are both incased in inert gases in airtight glass containers at the National Archives. Scientists are studying the feasibility of doing this for the Star-Spangled Banner, too. But the flag's grand size, over four stories high and weighing 300 pounds, presents special problems. For instance, how does a glass manufacturer produce two pieces of glass that BIG? The glass alone would weigh over seven tons!

Resources for Teachers

Barraclough, E.M.C., and W.G. Crampton. *Flags of the World*, London: Frederick Warne, Ltd., 1978.

Caffrey, Kate. *The Twilight's Last Gleaming: Britain vs. America, 1812-1815.* New York: Stein and Day, 1977.

Eggenberger, David. *Flags of the U.S.A.: An Illustrated History of the Stars and Stripes from Its Beginnings to the 50th Star.* New York: Thomas Y. Crowell Company, 1964.

Gebhart, John Robert. *Your State Flag.* Philadelphia: Franklin Publishing Company, 1973.

Guenter, Scot. *The American Flag 1777-1924: Cultural Shifts from Creation to Codification.* London and Toronto: Fairleigh Dickinson University Press, 1990.

Horsman, Reginald. *The War of 1812.* New York: Alfred A. Knopf, 1969.

Lord, Walter. *The Dawn's Early Light.* New York: W. W. Norton & Company, 1972.

Morris, Robert. *The Truth About the American Flag.* Beach Haven, New Jersey: Wynnehaven Publishing Co., 1976.

Suggested Books for Students

Browne, C.A. *The Story of Our National Ballads.* New York: Thomas Y. Crowell Company, 1960.

Kroll, Steven. *By the Dawn's Early Light: The Story of the Star-Spangled Banner.* New York: Scholastic Inc., 1994.

Miller, Natalie. *The Story of the Star-Spangled Banner.* Chicago: Childrens Press, 1965.

Spier, Peter. *The Star-Spangled Banner.* Garden City, New York: Doubleday & Company, Inc., 1973.

Answer Key

Flag Match, page 10

1. f, 2. b, 3. c, 4. d, 5. e, 6. a

Flag Questions, page 10

1. It represents the colonials willingness to strike back against the British, just as a coiled snake is ready to strike.
2. Iowa's state flag displays France's tri-color.
3. The Star-Spangled Banner had 15 stars in the canton; today's U.S. flag has 50. The Star-Spangled Banner had 15 stripes; today's U.S. flag has 13, just as the original flag did.
4. The pine tree represents the tree that the Sons of Liberty met under to plan various activities against the British occupation forces during the revolution.
5. It is the Zia Pueblo symbol of the sun, the source of all power.

Flag Quiz, page 13

1. Mary Pickersgill, 2. flag, 3. two, 4. $405.90; $168.54, 5. 30' x 42'; 17' x 25', 6. Fort McHenry, 7. $574.44

Beyond the Receipt, page 13

1. There are actually no written documents and little circumstantial evidence to prove that Betsy Ross sewed a flag for George Washington. Most historians do not believe the story is anything other than myth.
2. The receipt from Fort McHenry to Mary Pickersgill is hard evidence that she actually sewed the Star-Spangled Banner.

Flag Word Search, page 14

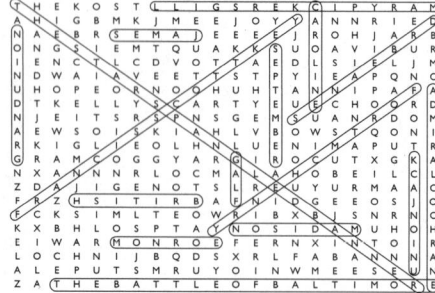

The Battle of Baltimore Map Test, page 18

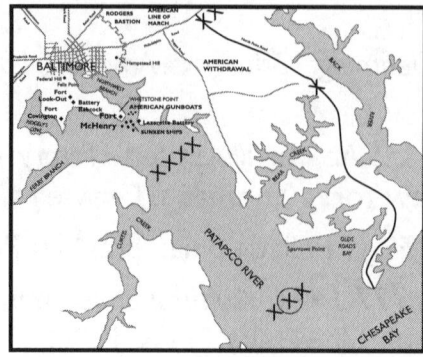

Matching, page 20

1. c, 2. b, 3. d, 4. a, 5. e

Key Questions, page 20

1. He had gone to get his friend released who was being held on British warships in the Chesapeake Bay. In the process of procuring the release, Key saw the British plans for attacking Fort McHenry, so the British wouldn't let Key go until after the bombardment was over.
2. British General Robert Ross
3. over 1500
4. Dr. Beanes had aided suffering British soldiers after the attack on Washington.
5. the Americans
6. Seeing the flag the morning of September 14, 1814, after the 24-hour bombardment of Fort McHenry knowing that the Fort had not fallen to the British naval and land forces.

Poem Questions, page 25

1. The broad stripes and bright stars of the flag
2. Fortifications used to protect
3. The British shells lobbed at Fort McHenry
4. The 15 stars in the canton
5. 15
6. 50 stars on today's flag, 15 on the Star-Spangled Banner
7. States admitted to the Union
8. 15
9. States admitted to the Union
10. Key was waiting on a truce ship as the events that were described in "The Star-Spangled Banner" unfolded. He saw the events personally.

11. "Anacreon in Heaven" was a British song.
12. March 3, 1931

Beyond the Anthem, page 25

1., 2. and 3. Answers will vary.

Blessed Be the Sacred Land, The National Anthem of Pakistan Review, page 27

1. Blessed be the sacred land, blessed be thou citadel of faith, The Order of the Sacred Land, This flag of the Crescent and the Star, Symbol of Almighty's protection.
2. By promising Pakistan to be the citadel of faith.
3. Answers will vary. Suggested answer, however: The Pakistan anthem sings about the broad virtues and values of Pakistan, while the American anthem describes the bombardment of a fort during a battle in a little remembered war.
4. Answers will vary. Suggested answer, however: Both anthems sing the praises of the native people of their countries and sing about lofty national hopes: Pakistan—May the nation, the country, and the state Shine in glory everlasting. United States—O're the land of the free and the home of the brave.

God Defend New Zealand, The National Anthem of New Zealand Review, page 29

1. God Defend New Zealand
2. 13
3. Answers will vary.
4. The mountains would be used like earthen ramparts, which protect by making it difficult to get to the enemy.
5. Answers will vary.
6. Answers will vary.
7. Answers will vary.
8. Answers will vary.